CHECK YOUR PRIVILEGE
Live into the Work

Myisha T

dirtpath
PUBLISHING

Alameda, California

Published in the United States by Dirt Path Publishing, Alameda, CA 94501
Contact for permissions or general inquiries - info@dirtpathpublishing.com
Contact for sales inquiries - sales@dirtpathpublishing.com

Printed in the United States
Cover Design: MT & CO
Cover Photographs: MT & CO, Candace Smith Photography
Internal Photographs: MT & CO
Text Design: MT & CO

First Edition

Trade paper ISBN 978-0-9905223-3-1
E-book ISBN 978-0-9905223-2-4

Library of Congress Cataloging-in-Publication Data

Hill, Myisha T.
Check Your Privilege: Leaning into the Work / edited by Myisha T. Hill. -- 1st ed.
ISBN 978-0-9905223-3-1(pbk)
. Relationships 2. Biography   3. Interpersonal Relations

DEDICATION

Dedicated to Women Around the World
Who Are Living Into The Work

CONTENTS

EDITOR'S NOTE by Myisha T   i

INTRODUCTION   v

I   ACCEPTING THE INVITATION INTO   1
ANTI-RACISM
by Britney Stafford

II   THE PRIVILEGE OF IDENTITY: 15
DEFINING BLACKNESS IN
PREDOMINANTLY WHITE SPACES
by Brandy Varnado

III   GETTING PROXIMATE   23
by Jennifer Kinney

IV   MODERATING MY PRIVILEGE   35
by Heather Anderson

V   NOBODY NEEDS A WHITE SAVIOR   51
by Jaime Blanco

VI   LIVING INTO THE WORK   61
by Myisha T

ABOUT THE CONTRIBUTORS   73

EDITOR'S NOTE

The world teaches us that if something has no value to us, it's easier to throw it away without any attempts of repair. My mission is twofold: to use my voice and experience to end throwaway culture and to keep white women accountable as their guide for living into their anti-racism journey. This journey serves to end unchecked privilege; by deepening relationships, we are better able to identify and do something about how power, privilege, and oppression affects the mental health of black and Indigenous women of color. To do this work is to be a co-conspirator for black and indigenous womxn of color.

What many well-meaning co-conspirators don't realize is that starting the journey into anti-racism requires a deep examination into the self. It is a journey similar to the hero's journey, allowing us to deeply uncover the roots of who we are in hopes of showing up differently in the world. The hero's journey in ancestor culture often involves fables of a hero who goes on an adventure, struggles through an existential crisis in order to overcome the crisis and learn the lessons, then returns home, all to begin a journey again.

The co-conspirator's journey is similar. It begins with awareness, followed by a call to action, and then requires us to face ourselves and our misdoings, including those that have brought us shame. The fear of shame can lead us to ghost the entire process, which is merely complicity in white supremacy racism. In order to be a true co-conspirator, we must turn the light on "shame" in order to sincerely grapple with the lessons we need to learn. Our victory is in the coming home to ourselves and our re-awakening. And then, we must go deeper, repeating the journey all over again.

It is my intention that this anthology will help all women on their co-conspired journeys because, unlike the traditional hero's journey, this journey is not done alone. We need each other, those like us and those different from us, because only when we recognize our common humanity, specifically as women and co-conspirators, can we take action to dismantle white supremacy racism together.

Myisha T

INTRODUCTION
Living Into the Work

Whether you are white or a Black, Brown Indigenous Person of Color (BBIPOC), "the work" is the process of dismantling one's relationships with patriacrical white supremacy. For BBIPOC it may look like decolonizing their relationship with systems of oppression and investigating their relationship with anti-blackness while learning to free themselves from the systems of oppression. For White folu it's taking the personal responsibility to name themselves as racists, work through their biases, and repair relationships they've knowingly or unknowingly damaged with the BBIPOC people in their lives, accepting personal responsibility for benefitting from and/or upholding racist ideas.

For all of us, "the work" is what we must do to start our journey toward becoming anti-racists.

In order to get started on this journey, myself, I had to grapple with the experiences of my youth. I grew up with a kind of special treatment from white suburban families who saw my family as a project, white folks who, in my experience, confused rescuing with relationship. Instead of asking what my family needed, they inserted themselves in our lives with financial gifts. While well-intentioned, these rescue moves were rooted in white saviorism, acts that "saved" us from the despair of our financial inequalities. By assuming they knew what my family needed instead of building solid relationships that would have allowed them to ask us, they dismissed both our self-determination and our humanity.

Further, the "colorblind" rhetoric of my suburban neighbors served to deny my relationship to slaves, forcing me to internalize my feelings and thoughts in order to assimilate into the dominant culture. I was careful not to speak Black Vernacular (African American Language), although most white males my age were into gangsta rap. I learned how to wear weaves in hopes of having hair like my peers. I never felt pretty enough because my hips were too wide, my breasts were too large, my hair never straight enough. I felt that my blackness was a curse, rather than a gift.

And, with all of this, I still had to stand strong as a proud, independent, black woman who took no shit. This left me struggling with a double consciousness, feeling the pressure to look at myself through the eyes of dominant culture and holding myself to their standards out of fear of being socially unacceptable, all while still trying to maintain my own identity.

This struggle continued for decades because my "work" could only begin when I was willing to examine my own relationship with anti-blackness, oppression, and white supremacy. Getting started required internal reflection, recognizing and naming my feelings and experiences through conversations, making deeper commitments to cross cultural community, and taking co-conspired action with others. If I want to shift the patriarchal, white supremacist narrative that has, thus far, resulted in the convergence of my shame and my culture, I must continue to live into the work.

Check Your Privilege pushes me to just this, vulnerably unbraiding of my culture from shame, to showing up as my full, authentic, and empathetic self, and providing a space for other people to do the same. I lead from a heart-centered space, using my story as a way forward to heal a collective. I lead from a mindful space of self-compassion, giving up the need to assimilate, and ending my own complicity in a white supremacist, capitalist, patriarchy.

I am not here to do the work; I am here to live into the work, something that requires a constant interrogation of my own motives and actions in relationship with white supremacy. Living into the work requires me to name my own racist behaviors, dismantle my relationship with patriarchy, and end my participation in throw-away culture. Living into that work requires me to accept that, even if white folks never fully dismantle their relationship with white supremacy, I can maintain relationships by trusting in the process of the work they are trying to do.

These are the relationships of co-conspirators, grounded in living into the work and bound by a sacred love language, one that requires an active state of accepting that the journey is not in our individual control. We are partners, trusting that we have one another's backs as we feel our way through our shadows, living in service to the knowing that we do so to dismantle the powers of oppression that hurt us all.

I: ACCEPTING THE INVITATION INTO ANTI-RACISM

by Britney Stafford

THE OPPORTUNITY

As a white woman on an anti-racism journey I can speak to a multitude of emotions that come with realizing that I don't know enough about systemic racism and white supremacist patriarchy as well as not doing enough to help dismantle it. If realizing, acknowledging, and learning to understand my complicity in a racist, white supremacist society is anything, it is emotional and uncomfortable.

I have felt deep anger and loathing towards myself, my family, my teachers, and society for participating in and perpetuating a sense of blissful disassociation from the subjugation of generations of people. I have felt gut-wrenching sadness and heartache for the countless black and brown people whose lives were, and still are, battered and stolen for the sake of upholding racist systems. These emotions and thoughts accompany me on this one step forward/two steps back anti-racism journey.

And, despite the challenges that come with living this work, accepting the faults and wrongs of myself and others has paved the way for growth, providing a liberation that can only come with knowing that living into the work brings an opportunity to learn and to change. When I began my journey into anti-racism work, I was certain that my personal experiences provided an already strong foundation as I knew what it meant to live in poverty and in underserved communities. What I didn't realize was things like immediately connecting poverty to black and brown people was a racist assumption.

While black and brown people are overrepresented in poverty, the detail always left out of my surface-level identification with people of color and the plight of poverty was that black and brown people are regularly and systematically held back based on the color of their skin, something that has never been true for me. As a white person my poverty was a matter of circumstance, not a disadvantage set before me at birth because of my race.

Further, being taught to be "color-blind" because "racism is bad" was not an automatic door to the teachings of anti-racism. I never learned about the existence of white privilege, nor did it ever call out my implicit and explicit biases or microaggressions towards black and brown people. The truth is, being raised as "colorblind" only kept me blind to the constant and systemic racism in the world around me. Even though I have lived through countless disadvantages and setbacks and suffered many hardships, none of these were ever a result of my white skin and it is simply fact that this sets me at an advantage over my black and brown counterparts.

And what about one of the nation's most shameful lies, that the "end of slavery" meant the end of racism in America? My education about slavery and racism did not teach me about the realities suffered for generations or the lies that encouraged and allowed for it. I wasn't taught about those who fought to keep black men, women and children enslaved or about how our government and legal systems still operate in a way that benefits white people while abusing and taking advantage of black and brown people. Instead, it taught me exactly what a racist, white supremacist society wants white people to believe: racism in America died with slavery and, therefore, racism is not a current societal problem that needs addressing.

How can racism not need addressing when chattel slavery lasted for more than 200 years? How about the fact that the Emancipation Proclamation was issued in 1863 and the ratification of the Thirteenth Amendment didn't come until the end of 1865? And then the truth that both these "victories" were soon made essentially moot by Jim Crow laws beginning at the end of Reconstruction in 1877 left unchecked until Brown v. Board of Education in 1954, almost 80 years later and the Civil Rights Act didn't occur for another 10 years after that, only 55 years ago. The end of slavery did not end racism and racism is not a figment of the imagination.

And, so, I came to a point where I had to make a choice: avoid the work of dismantling my own and societal white supremacy or take the opportunity to live into that work in both my own life and in the world.

STARTING MY JOURNEY
TOWARDS ANTI-RACISM

When I was twenty-seven, I took a new job that allowed me my first definitive glimpses of how systemic racism and white supremacy show up in our society. Through my work, I began to look deeply at the mental health treatment of black and brown women, which then led me to the broader subject of medical care for black and brown people. I was confronted with a disturbing reality of which I had previously been unaware: as a white person, I am more likely to receive attentive and humane care by those in the medical field than I would be if I were black or brown.

This privilege, to seek and receive competent care based on my needs, includes the ease of finding a large number of doctors in a variety of fields who don't hold specific biases towards me based on my white skin. Black and brown women, men, and children, however, are not only faced with wage discrimination which leads to inadequate finances and medical insurance, but they are also discriminated against by health care professionals who hold archaic and unsupported beliefs about their temperament, pain tolerance, and more.

This seemingly simple example of the systemic racism that exists in the medical industry served as one of the guiding forces that led me to my anti-racism journey, allowing me to begin to recognize so much of what I had, until that point, been totally unaware. Once my eyes began to open to the truth of racism and white supremacy patriarchy they could not be blind to it again. I continued research and reading in my free time, integrating what I learned into a new form of consciousness that was growing inside of me.

I need only do a cursory internet search to encounter an endless supply of information corroborating racially-biased abuses of power, discrimination, and acts of violence against black and brown people. I would bring what I learned into conversation with my husband and other acquaintances of mine. I would pause and reflect on how my life was shaped by these atrocities. I earnestly tried to consider the real impact of all of it on black and brown people, as well as other people of color, something I had to do not only because of my own whiteness but also, I would come to realize, because of the whiteness of the researchers who composed my sources of study. It took me a while to realize a large majority of the information I was reading was written by white people who, in many cases, made facing my complicity in a systemically racist society a little too easy for me to digest. While I had been learning a lot, I couldn't help but feel like I was missing so much by not focusing on the voices and experiences of those negatively impacted by racism and white supremacy: black and brown people and, more specifically, black women who experience discrimination at an intersectional level. As I reflected on this I began to realize that, while these white authors, scholars, and experts were insightful, they wrote in such a palatable way that made anti-racism work feel simple.

GETTING REAL

I slowed down my studies and made conscious decisions about focusing my learning through the lens of the lived experiences of POC, with a focus on black women. Around this time, I was also in the beginning stages of participating in a group created and guided by a black woman as a space for white women to explore how racism and white supremacist patriarchy shows up in ourselves, our families, and our communities. At first I wondered if I could handle the work, but after deciding I owed it to myself, my community, and every black and brown person now and previously living, I agreed to engage.

To my shock, I began to realize just how little I actually knew about racism and how deep it goes. Up until this point, I had been sharing articles and pictures on social media, fancying myself as an amateur Internet activist in service to bringing down white supremacy. Through my anti-racism work, however, I owned that, while well-intended, I never shared my own experiences or thoughts and I certainly wasn't owning any of my own racism. In fact not only did I not do it publicly; I didn't even do it privately.

I started learning new words and phrases I hadn't heard before. I was being made aware of the actions and inactions of myself and others. I was discovering the biases and lies black and brown people experience on a daily basis. I learned about how white fragility arises when white people are confronted with their own racist words or behaviors. I learned about the school-to-prison pipeline and the emergence of zero-tolerance policies in schools that continue to disproportionately penalize black students (including more school-related arrests and a higher likelihood to encounter the juvenile justice system and law enforcement). I began reading about the racial wage gap, hiring discrimination, and unequal education and career opportunities in the United States for nonwhite people. I thought about the widely accepted stereotype that black people are lazy and more prone to violence, which all stems from the terminology used historically to justify slavery and the excessive abuse against enslaved human beings.

Truthfully, this group was where my real work began.

MY DANCE WITH WHITE FRAGILITY AND GHOSTING

Ultimately I was confronted by the hard truth that throughout my life I had absorbed and nurtured my own racism, and that's when white fragility joined me on my anti-racism journey. White fragility refers to the uncomfortable feelings that arise in white people when faced with their own perpetuation of inequality and injustice. White fragility can also refer to the tendency of white people to become defensive when faced with these same things. And, in getting real with this group, I had to get real about my white fragility.

Allow me to introduce you to my White Fragility:

How dare people tell me I'm racist, I just can't believe it! Here I am putting in the hours, days, weeks, and months of my time to fight racism and white supremacy. That's automatically me NOT being a racist. I am a loving, caring and empathetic person. I can't be racist! Maybe I'm being too hard on myself, internalizing what I am learning about others. Them, not me. They are the racists.

Feeling angry and defensive, I wanted to lash out and blame everybody else. Instead of leaning into that discomfort and learning from it, I wanted to huff and puff at whoever or whatever was bringing me so close to my own racism. I wanted someone to blame so that I could be exempt from the work that was becoming too difficult, too uncomfortable.

Maybe, I told myself, I just needed a break. I deserve a break, I thought, because I had been working so hard on the subjects of racism and white supremacy and I needed a little time away. The reality was that I just couldn't handle facing my own ugly truths and I didn't want to admit that everything I was reading and learning also applied to me. I wasn't ready to come face to face with my own racism. How could I be ready to face that something as vile as racism was a part of who I am?

Cue ghosting. Ghosting is the act of abruptly halting communication with someone. Or in my case, no longer actively participating in my anti-racism work. I stepped back and focused on everything else, anything else. As my bruised ego healed, I shirked away from anything and everything that had to do with racism and anti-racism. Because without racism, there is no anti-racism, and when reading about one always led to the other, both ended up pointing to me as a complicit party that perpetuated white supremacy.

When this thought finally occurred to me, that I hadn't really been doing, feeling, living the work, what did I do? Did I slow down, acknowledge that truth, and go back to where I had left off? Nope. I gave into my anger, my doubt and my self-pity. Instead of actually feeling what was coming up for me, thinking through it and using that as a place to restart, I let my negative self-talk convince me that I couldn't do it anymore. Anti-racism was for someone stronger, someone with less baggage of their own to dig through. That wasn't me.

The more I told myself I couldn't do it, it was too hard and too uncomfortable, the easier it got to mentally pull away from my anti-racism journey. Days, weeks, months passed. But the thing about ghosting my anti-racism work is that I wasn't just disconnecting from the people, the movement, or the environment, I was disconnecting from a part of myself too. I wasn't allowing myself to address the issues I was having. I just wanted to ignore them and pretend they had gone away.

Since ghosting is the action of choosing to suddenly, and without explanation, cease involvement with a person or a situation, then ghosting anti-racism work is the perfect example of white privilege. When I ghost my anti-racism work I am saying that it isn't important enough for me to consider more seriously, let alone to consider more thoroughly. This is a way to avoid accountability, a pivotal tool in self-examination and anti-racism work.

When I ghost on my anti-racism work, I tell myself and others that the work has become too challenging for me. I don't want to be labeled as a bad person who quit on my anti-racism journey, so I just disappear because my recognition-hungry ego is feeling threatened. When I ghost, I tell myself and others that my comfort is more important than the collective inequality and injustice lived through by black and brown people every day. When I ghost I am not willing to accept my complicity, I am not willing to continue to learn how the exploitation of others benefits me, and I am not willing to own my racism.

These are the very reasons that ghosting anti-racism work is an exercise in white privilege: when the work gets hard I can choose to distance myself from it and focus on other things. Black and brown people do not have that luxury. Black and brown people can't not experience racism, discrimination, hatred, abuse, violence, and injustice. They do not have the privilege to ignore these crimes against themselves, their mothers and fathers, brothers and sisters, or their children.

Black people will always remember the generations before them who were forcibly bought, sold and enslaved, and they will not forget being segregated and classified as less than nor being murdered by the police. Indigenous people will not forget the rape and decimation of their bodies and land during and since the colonialism of this country. Japanese-American people will not forget the loss of their homes and businesses and being forced to live in American internment camps during World War II. Hispanic and Latinx people will not forget Mexican Repatriation, ICE raids, the immigration camps, and the separation of their families, or the public outcry for mass deportation and Trump's wall. Muslim and Middle Eastern people will not forget the Islamophobia caused by the "War on Terror" and the Muslim Travel Ban. The list goes on. And on. I have the advantage of being white in America, and with that comes the privilege of not being personally or intimately affected by any of this. Instead, I get to choose whether or not I will pay attention. I get to choose whether or not this is important to me. I get to choose how I show up in discussion and in the work. And ghosting on anti-racism work is simply no longer something I am willing to choose.

CONTINUING TO SHOW UP

When it comes to the fight for racial justice and lasting change, most of us want to be able to contribute to the conversation. We have fantasies about solving the world's problems, so we might live happy, healthy, fulfilling and peaceful lives; at some point after beginning our anti-racism journeys, however, we realize that this work requires a lot of self-exploration. And truthfully, we aren't always going to like what we find.

That. Is. Okay.

We have to hold ourselves accountable to this work, which means reflecting on our past thoughts and behaviors and facing our racist beliefs and actions. It is necessary to change ourselves before we can bring that change out into the world, and change is often scary and uncomfortable.

We all know that it can be really easy to say we are going to do something. It's not usually even difficult to even get started but continuing through self-revelations, difficulties, and discomfort is so hard. Anti-racism work is full of few personal highs and many personal lows because we all have shadows lurking around inside of us that will inevitably continue to show up during this work. And, let's be honest, reading about and experiencing the mental exhaustion and upsetting thoughts and feelings that come with anti-racism work doesn't exactly inspire us to roll up our sleeves and get started, let alone motivate us to continue.

This is where strength, compassion and empathy come in. One of the most helpful and important pieces of wisdom shared with me on this journey by a very patient guide is that, no matter how much progress I make and how long I have been doing this work, at some point I am going to screw up. I will get cocky, I won't get all of the facts straight, my inexperience will allow me to behave insensitively, or my determination will falter. Sometimes life will get in the way. After hearing that over and over again, I have begun to really listen and take it to heart.

There are times when guilt or shame make me question the work I am doing, and I am gently but firmly reminded that anti-racism work isn't a one-size-fits-all process. There is no definitive, proven-to-work-for-anybody method and there is absolutely not a set of instructions. This trial-and-error journey into self discovery, unlearning, and extensive reeducation is mine and mine alone. That is why it is imperative to this work that I remember, and keep reminding myself as many times and as often as necessary, that I am going to mess up, over and over again. But no matter how many times I fall, I have to keep going. I cannot allow myself to be held back by the realization that I have my own racism to acknowledge before I can do anything in my circles and my community, let alone this country and the rest of the world. I have to continue the work when it gets personal, difficult, and uncomfortable.

I am by no means done with this journey and I am certainly not perfect in my anti-racism work. I am still discovering previously unexplored beliefs. I am still unlearning a lifetime of racist stereotypes. I am still realizing just how deeply rooted racism is after centuries of exposure, absorption, and perpetuation. And as I process new information I am also coping with and trying to understand the emotions and reactions evoked in myself by this constant supply of traumatic, newfound knowledge.

My anti-racism journey means sometimes wanting to blame others and learning to understand where that knee-jerk reaction comes from. It means sometimes getting my feelings hurt and having my ego bruised from time to time. It means sometimes feeling too ashamed and overwhelmed to carry on. And it means carrying on anyway. I have felt so much on this journey so far and I have so much more to learn and grow through. Anti-racism work isn't easy; it is a purposeful, intentional examination and mindful learning of the truth.

II: THE PRIVILEGE OF IDENTITY
Defining Blackness in Predominantly White Spaces

by Brandy Varnado

I am unapologetically Black, with an emphasis on the unapologetic and Black. As a Black woman I am constantly confronting microaggressions, sexual fetishization, conscious and unconscious bias, and cultural prejudice in the workplace and other spaces. Colleagues are both uncomfortable around me and intrigued by me. It's not uncommon to be sitting in a meeting and receive a Gchat message that says "Wow! Love the hair," or to be asked by a White woman, "Is it okay if...?" they engage in some form of cultural appropriation.

These "compliments" and "asks" come at the expense of my intellect, an intellect that is further discounted in meetings where I am outnumbered, spoken over, cut off, or otherwise disregarded despite being well educated with degrees and certifications to match. When I assert myself or defend my contributions, I am told (not to my face of course), that I am being rude, aggressive or some code word for "unprofessional."

My ability to self-identify is also relentlessly challenged, with justifications for those challenges coming from the macro and the micro: White society's inability to confront its past and my colleagues' discomfort with who I am, what I look like, and how I choose to identify. This level of scrutiny essentially aims to tell me who I am and who I am allowed to be.

The constant need for me to reassert my humanity makes it both difficult and necessary to live in this work. Living in the work requires tools, skills, language, strength and the cultural capital that gives me access to the resources I need to defend and safeguard my identity. It's committing to participating in a relentless, two-pronged tug of war: to remain unapologetically Black and to defend my right to be unapologetically Black.

THE ABILITY TO SELF-IDENTIFY

When I enter into a workplace of well-meaning White folks and am corrected when I self-identify as Black, being told, instead, that I am a "woman of color," it calls me to live into the work.

To be honest, I still have trouble understanding how being "of color" is different from being "colored." In honor of my ancestors I take offense to being labeled "of color," as this label is limiting and dictates ownership in ways that repeats the violent and turbulent history of White supremacy that defines, teaches, and guides systems of oppression towards Black people in this country. The erasure of the word Black runs parallel with the attempt to erase Black narratives and Black culture from White spaces.

Beyond the label itself, being corrected about the identifier I chose for myself is demeaning. My ability to self-identify does not and should not require prior, written or expressed consent from the gatekeepers of White Supremacy, no matter how well-intentioned they think they are.

CONFRONTING MY OTHER SELF

My work as an educator has taught me a constant stream of uncomfortable lessons not only about race and the impact our implicit bias has on the work we do, but also on our relationships with one another and ourselves. Institutional White supremacy runs so deep that public and private call-outs against my Blackness is not done just by my white colleagues, but by other Black people as well.

When I was younger, I looked forward to starting my career as a teacher in a space where there were other Black faces, people who had more experience and credentials from whom I could learn. I quickly learned, however, that in most cases this sense of community was a façade. My experience has been that Black brothers and sisters in public spaces are quick to shut me down, disassociating with me if I intentionally or unintentionally subvert the status quo.

Once I was told by a Black colleague, "Sis, I can't believe you're wearing braids, you're bold." As if there is some universal oath we take when entering corporate America that says "all things Black must go!" Another instance occurred while sitting in a meeting advocating on behalf of Black children. My co-worker tapped me on the shoulder, offering me "the look" that says, "Sis, you're going too far." Deflated at once again having my passion and knowledge moderated by others, I closed off emotionally and struggled to show up as my authentic self for sometime. I have been left on the battlefield for my people by my people many times and I cannot readily say that I have healed from the trauma of those experiences.

In recent years I have had several difficult conversations with Black co-workers about how, all too often, Black people uphold inherently racist systems of oppression and how veteran Black employees fail to be mentors, negating the possibility of a Black community existing in White organizations. Their responses to my concerns were as bleak as my hope for greater commonality saying, in essence, "Well, you know how it is." I did not know. In fact, I was confused. I was raised to believe that Black people would love and support each other when no one else would. I grew up witnessing strong examples of this, but the sense of community and racial solidarity did not exist for me in this space. These are things that are not explained or stated outright; they become part of the hidden curriculum that one can only learn through experience.

I know now my will to remain Black and proud of my identity is both important and revolutionary, especially as an educator because schools are where young people come to learn about themselves and the world around them. Showing up authentically communicates truth and vulnerability in a way that allows students to do the same and this is important if education is ever to be transformational for our children.

RACE VIS A VIS EDUCATION

Education remains one of the most segregated institutions in

America, despite the landmark decision to desegregate schools via Brown v. Board of Education in 1954. The teaching force is still largely White and female and students who are at or near the bottom of every measurable success outcome are largely Black. The racial achievement gap, renamed the "wealth gap" (see what they did there?) continues to grow, leaving Black students further behind than any other race.

Whenever I raise issues of concern about Black children suffering in an education system with a school to prison pipeline made stronger depending on zip code, the conversation quickly gets redirected by non-Blacks who grow uncomfortable having to face their complicity for remaining silent, conveniently ignoring the root problem of white supremacy because they either don't know what to do or they simply don't care.

Many of the educators who cry when they come to recognize that children are, in fact, being left behind are the same educators who have argued that Black students are incapable of or uninterested in learning, almost never acknowledging their failure to engage these students in the learning. Instead of grappling with these truths, someone speaks to progress being made in the Latino community, another calls for greater support for English learners, and another defends the plight of undocumented students. The opportunity to have a real conversation about the persistent and predictable plight of Black students in our schools is lost, over and over again.

IN CONCLUSION

By being Black, identifying as Black, and embracing my Blackness, I am subverting a system that often claims I do not exist. I am grateful for the allies who refuse to be bystanders and address issues of prejudice and discrimination as they arise. And we have to do better.

We have to move past good intentions and begin to do the work that ignites radical change and make an impact. Instead of interrupting me to say, "what I think she means to say is...," I would appreciate allies who instead say "let her finish, she can speak for herself." I would appreciate this more than a text, email or sidebar in the hallway saying, "I'm sorry that happened to you," "they were wrong", "I can't believe they said that." While well-intentioned, it's only said in private and, frankly, too little, too late.

I want Black people to not be ashamed of being called Black and exhibiting their culture in the workplace even if it is at the chagrin of others. We must remain vigilant; our presence is decreasing as Brown becomes the New Black and, if we wield away our power by not claiming our language, our culture and our place in these spaces, we eradicate ourselves. Let us continue to communicate our needs and build community because this is what it takes.

This is living into the work. It is reclaiming our identity, speaking our truth through the lens of all that we are, and doing so unapologetically.

III: GETTING PROXIMATE
by Jennifer Kinney

Sunlight flooded the bathroom, where I sat with my mother. Light bounced wildly through the window to the mirror above the sink and illuminated everything from my little white cotton dress with its hand-sewn eyelets to the whites of my mother's eyes. It's been close to 40 years since she took me into my grandparent's bathroom for that "serious talk," but I remember the day like it was yesterday.

She hoisted me onto the toilet and put her face right in front of mine. "Where did you hear that song?" she asked. Her eyes were a mix of sadness and anger. She wanted to know how and why her sweet little four-year-old was singing a rendition of eeny, meeny, miny, moe, that replaced tiger with the n-word.

"Grandma!" I squeaked in my little four-year-old voice. "Grandma sings that song to me!" She drew a deep, almost resigned breath and explained to me that some people, even people I loved, could say horrible and hateful things. She taught me that the "n-word" was a vile and dehumanizing word and that it was unacceptable for me to use it.

It was my first lesson on racism as well as my first realization that people I loved and looked up to could say and do horrible things.

A year before this incident, my parents had packed up our tiny house in the city and took off for the countryside. The countryside afforded them a larger home and more land at a fraction of the cost. They were able to leave the confines of city life, filled with nosy neighbors and family members who were a little too close for comfort, and trade it in for the quiet seclusion of a life lived in the woods. It was as close to the middle of nowhere as we could get without going off-grid, and it was their dream come true.

I grew up in what I considered the average American household minus the fun that living in a more populated area could offer. When we first moved to the countryside, there were no traffic lights, medical facilities, or fast-food restaurants; and the running joke was that we'd know it was time to leave after the first stoplight was installed. Things have changed a lot over the last forty years, but the one thing that hasn't is the racial makeup of the town.

I didn't think much about the racial makeup of my hometown when I was growing up. One black family lived in the area, and for most of us, this was proof of racial progress. I assumed few people of any race would choose to live in such a boring place. Add that naïveté to a heavy dose of historical ignorance about the modern-day relevance and impact of segregation and redlining, and it's fair to say I was simply "racially stupid" (to quote Crystal Fleming, author of How To Be Less Stupid About Race).

Still, if you had asked the young me if I was an anti-racist back then, I would have given an emphatic "yes!" I stood proudly on the idea that I was opposed to racism. I attended diverse private schools closer to the city. The stories I learned in school from the Civil Rights era inspired me. I saw Dr. King, Rosa Parks, and other freedom fighters as personal heroes. My favorite authors were Toni Morrison and Maya Angelou. My first love and serious boyfriend was Black. I had a reputation for confronting racism, and my friends knew that if anyone uttered racist words in my presence, I would speak up. In my mind, I was the model anti-racist.

It wasn't until the last six or seven years, that I began to dig deep into anti-racism work and realize just how wrong I had been. The more I moved toward real anti-racism, the more I learned how far away I'd been from it. The untangling and subsequent deconstruction from decades-long racist messaging has been a journey involving many different experiences, the culmination of which opened me to a greater understanding of white supremacy and the daily realities of racism that exist today.

LIVING ABROAD

I can then look back over my life and identify several other core moments that led to my deconstruction and current anti-racism activism. Moving abroad, while not the first, was one of the most critical moments in my journey. In 2007, my husband and I packed up our lives and headed to Shanghai, China. We were eager to immerse ourselves and learn as much as we could about Chinese traditions, history, food, and culture, and we felt ready for the challenge. We sensed we were moving into something that would be as beautiful as it would be difficult, but neither of us realized how much it would teach us about our own culture and identity or the way it would reshape the way we approach the world.

Living in China as a foreigner was equal parts excitement and difficulty. As a result, the expatriate community is well established and tightly knit. Things that would typically draw people to one another -- life experience, income level, and shared interests -- were secondary to the shared experience of being an expat in China. This gave us a unique opportunity to build friendships with people from all over the world and all walks of life

Living in a foreign country has a way of teaching lessons that are difficult to come by when all of our creature comforts surround us. In its most obvious way, living as a foreigner exposes us to other cultures, but it can also reveal our arrogance, ignorance, and naiveté. The exposure and relationships I had with such a diverse group of people gave me insight into how my culture had shaped and formed me. I learned how it influenced the way I saw the world, including how I parented, viewed marriage and family, approached people on the street, engaged with politics, purchased food at the grocery store, and invited others into my home.

REPATRIATING

I returned to the U.S. with a deep curiosity. My experience abroad opened me to wonder, allowing me to hold my beliefs with greater humility and to seek understanding and connection among differences. It was the perfect primer in many ways for my antiracism journey.

One year after repatriating to the U.S., Trayvon Martin was killed. This event was the single most impactful moment on this journey. I'll never forget the first time I heard Trayvon's mother speak. I couldn't help but think of my children and what it would be like to be in her place. It haunted me. The subsequent media coverage and the conversations that took place across the nation also made me realize there was a much larger problem than I understood.

The reading, watching, and listening I did about the trial and the issues that surrounded it started to chip away at the layers of stuck-on thinking and racist narratives I had absorbed since childhood. I learned that I didn't know anything when it came to the experiences of Black Americans. I also learned that there was a tremendous amount of injustice, pain, and division. I saw that racism was alive and well and rearing its ugly head in the form of public opinion over the murder of Trayvon, a teenage boy killed for wearing a hoodie while black. Pulled from the comfort of my ignorance, I began to feel restless in my Michigan suburb.

Two years after the murder of Trayvon, my husband and I decided we needed a change so we decided to leave the suburbs and move to Detroit. When people heard we were moving to Detroit, we got a lot of blank stares. Some people seemed genuinely excited and interested, while others appeared confused and concerned. "Detroit?" "Why would you want to move to Detroit?" We heard every trope possible. People would ask about the crime in the city, comment on the "mismanagement and corruption in the government," lament the failing schools and bring up mayor Kwame Kilpatrick. They would talk about the '67 uprising (people from the suburbs refer to it as a riot), the state of many neighborhoods, and talked about thecity as though its struggle and perceived ruin rested squarely on the shoulders of the people of Detroit, namely the Black community.

Those who were excited and interested were usually people caught up in the Detroit "comeback story." There was a time when I was a part of that group, but the more I learned, the more problematic and complex I realized it was. The whitest gentrification has been taking place in the blackest city in the United States, and few people outside the city have had the understanding or courage to discuss it or the devastation it was bringing. Some people are happy to drive in from the suburbs, flocking to all the new hot spots; but on their way to their $10 lattes, $60 yoga classes, and $15 cocktails, they are stepping on decades of established communities. Moving into my new predominantly Black neighborhood as a white woman was equal parts openness, cluelessness, and arrogance. I had no hesitation in moving; after all, I wasn't a racist. What was telling was the fact that I had no understanding nor appreciation for how my neighbors might be impacted by my white family moving into their community. It never occurred to me that my presence as a white woman might make my Black neighbors feel uncomfortable. As I was learning about the differences between police presence in white communities and policing in Black communities, stories readily emerged about white people, especially women, calling the police on Black people. Their offenses ranged from barbecuing and going to the pool, to taking baby photos and merely existing. As I was putting all of this together, I had to ask myself why I felt comfortable moving into my neighborhood without thinking about the impact of my presence? Why didn't I know that my whiteness could cause fear and concern for my Black neighbors? The only thing I focused on communicating was that I didn't have a problem living among Black people, and that revealed a deeply held belief that I saw whiteness as harmless and blackness, something to be feared. All of this was, at its core, white supremacy.

While living in China played a pivotal role in understanding culture and realizing how much tradition, belief, and attitude is shaped by forces that remain virtually invisible, moving to Detroit brought a level of reality and connection only proximity could bring. I had a lot to learn about history, context, and my own implicit bias.

First, I learned about the narratives I had absorbed and adopted, as well as the beliefs I held without realizing them. Second, I learned that the ideas I held were rooted in arrogance and assumption. Third, I learned that these ideas were part of a more sinister racist narrative that was deeply rooted in the belief that Black people were inherently corrupt and incapable. As I began to learn more about the real history of segregation and redlining, the simmering racial tensions, Detroit's uprising in the 60s, and white flight, I learned why the narrative I had absorbed, held, and even shared, was so deeply problematic.

Moving to Detroit exposed just how clueless I had been. I thought I had a phenomenal education, even fancied myself a bit of a history geek. I was familiar enough with the civil rights movement, but I believed it to be a bygone era. In my mind, it was part of a rectified and distant past. Upon hearing my neighbor's stories, however, this distant history became close and personal and put a human reality to what I had read about in books. A number of my neighbors were alive during Jim Crow. Some had stories of marching, while others saw Dr. King give speeches in real-time. Several of my neighbors had grandparents who had been enslaved. My neighbor's mother, like many in her generation, would only drive along the surface streets because she was afraid of getting pulled over on an isolated highway where she might be hurt by those who said their job was to protect.

As the complexity and reality of this history came to life through the people around me, I realized how ignorant I had been. These realizations propelled me into studying history more. I realized how insulated I had been in predominantly white spaces, and how incredibly arrogant my assumptions and beliefs of a post-racial society were. Life began to make a lot more sense once I started learning about the historical construction of race the hundreds of years of resulting attitudes, political views, scientific theories, and laws rooted in racism that legitimized the dehumanization of Black people and other people of color.

Living life among my neighbors, going to neighborhood meetings, and getting to know people in local politics has had the greatest impact on my journey toward anti-racism. It has allowed me insight into life that no textbook could provide. It has given me insight into the jewel that this city is. At the same time, it helped me realize how internalized my racism was having lived a life nestled in the womb of segregation, redlining, racism, as well as its effects on my entire life.

WHAT'S NEXT

When I started this work in 2012, I had no idea how much liberation I needed and how much living in proximity would reshape my understanding and view of what it means to live an anti-racist life. Over the last six years, I have learned a lot about what it looks like to live into the work. I have been listening and learning from Black educators and am developing the language I need to understand racism and better engage dialogue with the white people around me. When I first started, I made the common mistake of focusing on what I could go out and do to "fix" things, but I have learned that the most important work came once I focused on myself.

Focusing primarily on my internal work over the last several years has allowed me to observe, learn, and deconstruct a lot of the subtle racist messaging I had consumed growing up as a white woman in the U.S. Living into the work has required an honesty, vulnerability, and commitment that has led to so much personal freedom and joy.

IV: MODERATING MY PRIVILEGE
by Heather Anderson

COMPLICIT NO MORE

I'm white and grew up in a wealthy, predominantly white suburb in the Bay Area of California. I never learned about racism and my role in it because I didn't have to.

In junior high, I had one black friend, April*, the only black girl in the school. We were best friends and hung out together in the "bad kid" crowd, all of us connected by our various feelings of not belonging. We mostly bonded over riding skateboards, crushing on the same boys, smoking cigarettes, and taking care of the sheep we adopted together through 4H.

During those years I was often in trouble and it wasn't uncommon for the principal, a white man, to give me a "pep talk" to try to get me back on the right track. He'd say: "I know you're not a bad kid, but you're hanging around with the wrong crowd," which only made me dig in harder and cling to those friends more dearly. It was an obviously superficial and biased judgment. This principal didn't know me or know that I was any "better" a kid than the others. I don't recall him ever calling April into the office for the same kind of talk.

April didn't end up enrolling in the local high school so, as it happens with friends in adolescence, we lost touch. I had an uninformed sense that feeling 'othered' might have contributed to why she left, but I never spent real time thinking about how her race might have played a part in determining her future. My whiteness afforded me the privilege of not needing to.

Through high school and my twenties I thought I knew all there was to know about white supremacy. "White suprema-cists" sported shaved heads, had swastika tattoos, or waved con-federate flags. "Racism" was defined by overt, individual acts by "bad" white people - obvious things, like using racial slurs, exclusion, or even violence. I never thought of myself as a racist, but I must admit to being complicit in what felt like the gray area of "good people" saying racist things to one another in jest, silently cringing when I should have put a stop to it.

I never saw the invisible systems conferring dominance on white people from birth because from my frame of reference, especially at that age, I just thought that's the way life was. As Peggy McIntosh wrote, "My schooling gave me no training in seeing myself as an oppressor, as an unfairly advantaged per-son, or as a participant in a damaged culture." It didn't occur to me that me getting ahead meant that, in the system we have, others were left behind.

It's baffling to look back and see how long I managed to remain ignorant. It took the combination of becoming a mother and listening to the emotional pain of a close friend to really snap me out of my stupor. I'm seeing everything now in retrospect in an attempt to be someone who actively examines and disman-tles my own biases, and who uses my white privilege to combat racial inequality.

YOUTHFUL COWARDICE

After four years at a racially and ethnically homogenous high school, I went on to attend the University of California at Davis, a place only slightly more diverse overall with a central quad, the hub of the campus, completely segregated by race and ethnicity. The white and Asian-American students sat predominantly in one area, the black students in another, and the international students in another. It didn't feel right, but I wasn't sure how to bridge the gap. I didn't feel like I could just walk across the grass and sit at a table of strangers. Further, the circles I traveled in -- the marching band, the Crew team, the Salsa club, and people majoring in German Lit -- offered me little connection to people much different than me, particularly students who were black.

As a music major, I sought out places to engage in music all over campus, and when I met someone who told me they were in the UC Davis Gospel Choir, I felt really excited. I'd grown up singing in choirs and in children's musical theater and really craved that choral experience as an adult. I lacked the background for the religious aspect of this choir and there were only two other white members, the rest of the 250-member choir being students who were black, so I felt nervous about joining, wondering if it was a good fit for me.

I didn't know then the concept of cultural appropriation or that I should appreciate the necessity for preserving safe spaces for people of color to commune and create a sense of belonging, I just wanted to sing. A student who was black encouraged me and said it was open to all students, no matter my religion or race, so I signed up. Normally I'm pretty extroverted, but I noticed immediately how shy and out of place I felt as the minority. The feeling of looking different from everyone in the room gave me empathy for what it might feel like to live with those kinds of ratios in other areas of life and school. I felt a lurking anxiety and an irrational feeling that I wouldn't be accepted or welcome because of my whiteness even when, in reality, everyone I met was incredibly welcoming and kind.

At the top of each choir practice, I'd stand around awkwardly silent or making pathetic smalltalk — desperate for class to get started. I was nervous to engage in friendship for fear I might not get cultural references, inside jokes, and, most worrisome, that I'd accidentally say something offensive. And then we'd sing together. It'd be suddenly intimate, moving, communal, soulful and glorious.

When the music ended, we'd go our separate ways.

On our first field trip together, carpooling out of town for a performance in a Baptist church, we were all excited. We were in the timid beginnings of friendship and I was starting to feel more comfortable. I'd never been to a Baptist sermon before and found myself mesmerized and moved by the Pastor's booming voice and charismatic delivery. He had us all out of our chairs, yelling, clapping and crying out a gleeful "Amen!" The energy was palpable and I was inspired.

The pastor then started talking about taking the "high road" and used the analogy of driving a car and not letting the devil ride in the backseat. I was fully with him and feeling his message until that message took a a turn and I realized that the "devil" was a metaphor for people who are gay. I felt gutted.

On the ride home I nervously asked the five students in my van if anyone else had felt uncomfortable with that analogy. No one said anything. There was a long, awkward silence. Then the one Jewish guy in the van said, "It's sad, but you gotta just roll with it."

Why did I assume that no one else in the choir secretly felt like me? I'd only asked the five people in my van. What might have happened if I'd viewed the choir as 250 individuals and not like a falsely homogenous monolith? Maybe I could have found and made friends who shared my discomfort but enjoyed the music and positive messages enough to stick with it and seek change? If I'd been in a group of 250 white people, I might have felt more willing to speak out, ask questions, and poll for like-minded friends. Feeling already like an outsider, my courage to rock the boat was nil.

It was misguided of me to assume, based on my assumptions of race and religion, that everyone supported the pastor's beliefs that I found problematic. Instead of daring to engage deeply about things that matter with people who were starting to become my friends, I let fear win. I let my assumptions win. I let my racism win.

I dropped out of the choir. I see this now as a double-failure for social justice: My failure to stand up for the LGBTQIA population and my failure to trust that I could open this dialogue and create deeper, more meaningful connections with my fellow students of color.

THE ELEPHANT IN THE WORKPLACE

After college, I spent over a decade working for my dad at a private bank he founded in San Francisco. Outside of the glaring privileges of being white, having a college degree, and the nepotism factor of being the CEO's daughter, there was at least an improvement in the number of friendships I was able to develop with black colleagues.

I'd still never heard the term "white privilege" but I began to feel and see it in action as I experienced an easier path up the ladder than my colleagues. Because I had a college degree, I was already a step ahead of much of the staff, something that made me consider that we might be shuttled down a certain path from birth. I noticed my own frustrations in the banking world around male privilege and sexism and saw them multiplied for people of color, particularly black women of color. Though I could clearly see this racist patriarchy in place, we didn't discuss racism at work, just as we didn't discuss sexism.

We were so busy being polite, so afraid to say the "wrong things," that nothing was said at all.

THE WAKE-UP CALL

It wasn't until I became a mom and made a dear new mom-friend who was black, that I got what I needed to shake me awake to the possibility that I was not only bypassing white supremacy, I was contributing to it.

When I met Cameron* we'd both just had our first babies. I was instantly drawn to her because she'd done everything I'd liked to have done if I'd made different choices: she'd been a journalist, majored in business, and traveled. It was insta-love. I added her and several other mothers from our breastfeeding group to a Facebook group I started so we could stay connected - a group that would grow to become "The Mamahood," and the beginning of my social justice education.

During the insane infant and toddler stages, she was one of the few people I managed to hang out with in real life consistently and someone I considered a true friend. Not only did we have many things in common, it turned out that our first babie both grew to have similar special needs, which bonded us even further.

As the years quickly swept by, this small group grew to an online chat forum for mothers all over the Bay Area and I ran it in the only way I knew how: keeping the vibes high, "friendly," and "polite." If there was something rude or possibly racist, I'd delete it. If an argument about anything broke out, including race, I'd clean it up. Delete! Delete! It looked to be what other mom group moderators were doing as well so it felt like not only the easy way, but also the right way.

As it turns out, I was perpetuating the crisis of white "politeness" - an ill-conceived notion by the dominant culture that above all else, we must be polite to each other especially when it allows institutionalized racial injustice to remain the organizing principle of the day.

The first time a conversation about race really blew up in the group, we had grown to about 6,000 members. I realized I had no skills with which to intervene, but knew in my gut that it wasn't something I could just delete. I called on my friend, Cameron; she had been in the group since day one and I trusted her implicitly.

"What should I do or say?" I asked her.

The conversation that followed changed everything for me. Apparently, she'd been frustrated for six years, holding pent up anger and disappointment with how I ran the group. I was shocked as she explained that deleting things that "felt ugly" actually silenced conversations that needed to happen and people who needed to be heard. People should get to respond in anger when something is unjust, racist, or ignorant. Nobody ever benefits from me sweeping vitriol, nor the pain it causes, under the rug.

Who knew? She did. I didn't.

While her advice sounded good in theory, my knee-jerk reaction was to panic because if I didn't delete these conversations, I'd have to moderate them. I'd have to learn what to say and how to say it. I knew literally nothing about discussing racism and the thought of it was terrifying. So much resistance welled up in me: It was going to require ten times the moderating hours. I have five kids, three of them at that point weren't yet able to dress themselves. The group was already an overwhelming volunteer project. More than anything, I was sure I'd fuck it up.

"I don't feel safe in your group and never have," Cameron said.

That was the slap-in-the-face I needed to buck up and at least try. And, while she didn't say so, I'm guessing she also resented feeling like it was her job as my black friend to teach me these things. I'd never bothered to learn about racism and she, someone who I considered to be my close friend, had no choice but to live and breathe it.

I decided to take on this problem full-speed and moved on a plan to get a quick education about racial justice, equity, and what it means to create a truly safe space for marginalized members. I started googling and got to work training our moderators. I told them that we were no longer deleting "ugly" threads if they pertained to topics of social justice.

Instead of deleting, we'd now need to stay on top of conversations for hours, sometimes days. We'd allow the conversations to happen but not without publicly confronting problematic comments. We wanted members to know that, while we allow the ignorant and offensive comments to remain, that they were not acceptable and we were only leaving them public so that others could learn from the responses. If we spotted examples of whitesplaining, tone policing, or anything of the like, we'd point that out as well, providing definitions and links to related resources. Our intentions were to keep the dialogue and issues out in the open, honor voices that need to be heard, and offer resources for those who were willing to engage.

I asked members who were willing to let me know what they needed from me. When I opened myself up to feedback, the initial wave was filled with the same pent up frustration and anger as that of Cameron. It was as if the realities of racism that I'd ignored for years in my rearview mirror were now suddenly standing in front of me in the middle of the road.

My instincts were to feel defensive in the face of their anger. I felt like the criticism of my past behavior was unfair because I hadn't known better. I cried from exhaustion. I felt near-constant stress.

In truth I was drowning in white fragility, both my own and that of others. White people were constantly angry at me, sending me private text messages every time we allowed them to be "called out," or when we kept a thread open that contained discord or angry, race-related conversation.

"Why are you racist towards white people?"

"Why have you let this support group for moms fill up with 'hateful' dialogue?"

"Why is discussing race allowed in a mom's group?"

"Why do you allow such 'negativity'?"

"I thought this was supposed to be an uplifting 'support' group'?"

"Race is an inextricable part of motherhood," I'd respond, "so discussing personal experiences of racism is completely appropriate in a mom's group." When asked why we allow people to argue, sometimes aggressively, I'd explain that the alternative is to silence the conversations and we won't do that anymore because these are important conversations that need to be had. I'd say all that, and then I'd go to bed feeling doubt, dread, defeat.

Further, I found that people of color were not feeling particularly honored by us allowing angry, heated conversations filled with ignorance and fragility because the conversations, while important, were also requiring vast amounts of their emotional labor and, in turn, causing them harm.

I realized it's actually impossible to gain a "quick education" in anti-racism. And while all the googling and inquiring is a beginning, true anti-racism work takes deep introspection, internal work, and time for integrating that work into practice. We continued to evolve our knowledge and skills as well as creating better-defined boundaries, scripts, and a glossary of terms.

I often felt completely overwhelmed because the more I learned, the more I realized I had left to learn. It was easy to feel like the whole effort was hopeless. There was even a time when I publicly violated my own guidelines by accidentally tone policing a member without realizing it. It took six angry members telling me off - and me trying my best to listen - until I could even understand what I'd done wrong. I had to accept that engaging in a co-learning experience means people, myself included, are going to make mistakes as we attempt to undo our own internalized issues.

CONFRONTING MY OWN FRAGILITY

A new member, a woman of color, posted within just a few minutes of joining that she was deeply disappointed by her experiences with how topics dealing with race are handled in "mom groups" and that she hoped this group would be different. I wanted to cry out, "Give us a chance! We're different! We've been working so hard here!" But before I could respond, the thread grew out of control with defensive, insensitive, fragile responses of white members. And angry sentiments of POC members who'd missed the work we'd done, validating this criticism.

Before I could defensively toot our own horn, the comments proved how far we still needed to go. Then Cameron, who'd been largely inactive in the group since our conversation, angrily chimed in that she felt the same way. Further, she said, this group was no different.

I had grown a thick skin to the criticism of strangers; Cameron was my friend and this felt personal. And only when things feel personal are we really going to do the work to grow.

After some time and much reflection, I now see the problem between Cameron and me wasn't about me not working hard to remedy something she identified as a problem; it was about my failure to see that I couldn't enact a "quick fix" to dismantle white supremacy, in my group or anywhere beyond. I'd failed to dig deeper, to do my own inner work so that I could begin to lead others on the journey or create a truly safe space.

I realized the work was never going to be perfect or pretty. It was never going to look like progress in a nice straight line to an end destination. It was going to be cyclical, sloppy, messy. Sometimes it was going to be heartbreaking.

EVOLVING

It took years of being educated by women of color, both bluntly and gently, for being complicit in silencing conversations, for being slow to take action, for not doing enough, for taking years to produce Social Justice Guidelines for engagement in the group, for not having a diverse moderator team...before I stopped feeling defensive.

To evolve, I had to step outside of myself and lose my ego. I needed to let go of my desire to be liked, or my need for approval from the crowd. I also needed to let go of my fear of failing publicly, for being called out in front of a large audience, and of looking like a fool. I had to release any perfectionist tendencies or pride around being perceived as some kind of infallible leader who has all the answers. Instead of leading from a podium I now want to use my platform to amplify the voices of those who have done their inner work and are ahead of me on this journey.

The work is not about me and this support group, it's about much bigger things - like legitimate rage stemming from racist systems at play in our society at large. What I can do is build my own education, share my resources, keep listening, learning and staying open. I can build real friendships with women of color in my personal and professional lives. I can draw boundaries and hold expectations for members of The Mamahood. I can be empathetic and lead by example.

It's not going to be beautiful. It's not always going to be peaceful. And I'm going to constantly make mistakes. Accepting these facts was a relief because I no longer felt like I had to be perfect to be working towards progress.

*names were changed for privacy purposes

V: NOBODY NEEDS A WHITE SAVIOR

by Jaime Blanco

COMING TO KNOW WHAT I DIDN'T KNOW

I was born to kind, hardworking, generous, down-to-earth parents in Ann Arbor, Michigan. We come from a white, midwestern, Evangelical Christian background where, both in word and deed, kindness, honesty and helping others were essential to our upbringing. My father was always pulling over to help strangers on the side of the road and my mother, who has worked at a local nursing home for decades, always taught us to look for ways to help others.

I arrived in East Oakland when I was 22 years old with a bachelor's degree in Social Work and Psychology, a couple of internships worth of work experience, and way too much certainty. As a midwestern Christian, the certainty I had in God's love and truth, as well as my ability to offer that love and truth to a world that needed it, was a part of my cultural DNA. After all, we're midwestern Christians! We know some things.

What we don't typically know is how very little we usually know. For one, I always thought my hometown was very diverse because I had grown up with a few friends of a different race. I didn't realize how my world had been almost exclusively white until I started living in a place that wasn't.

I really did want to help others and do the right thing; the problem was so much of what I believed about "the right thing" was guided by my upbringing, culture, and privilege. Despite what I had been taught, the "right thing" isn't always clear or obvious. No one told me how complex this world can be.

After graduating from college I came to Oakland for a one-year volunteer program which recruits young adults to do a year of service while exploring faith, poverty, injustice and racism. Individuals are placed on a team and live in the same community they serve. During my college years I knew I wanted to make a difference and I also knew I didn't want a traditional suburban life. I needed to live a life reflective of my values and this volunteer program seemed to offer me just that.

I began my year of volunteering, primarily with folks who were African American. I volunteered at a local high school and another youth outreach program and ended up forming what would become life-long relationships that made me want to stay in Oakland long term. After my stint as a volunteer I was hired by a non-profit foster care agency which trained me to do therapeutic mentoring with foster care youth and I did this work for many years while continuing to mentor youth from the community.

My true passion, then and now, focuses on walking alongside youth and families in my East Oakland neighborhood. In those early days a few friends and I started hosting a small group of youth from families with which we had formed close relationships. There was a lot of chaos in our neighborhood and in the lives of the youth in our care and we wanted to make sure, for a few hours at least once a week, they could focus on themselves and reflect on God, life, and relationships. We created a space where our youth could come together to grow and find support from both adults and one another.

Humbled quickly by our inadequacies as we realized our youth faced obstacles way bigger than we could "fix," it was not too long before I realized that my life had been so different from the youth in our care. As a teen, my basic needs were met. My life never felt in danger. I did not face systemic and personal racism and other forms of bias in my daily life. For the first time I came to understand that the "right thing" for me was not the same "right thing" for others, if for no other reason than our life circumstances and experiences were totally different.

I did not realize how much my privilege increased my ability to go to college and then take a year to volunteer before starting my career. I was never aware of all the resources I had nor the obstacles I never had to face. Neither cookie-cutter Christianity nor self-help recipes could uncomplicate the potentially life-altering decisions our youth faced every day. The longer I work with youth, the more I realize they do not need preaching or "experts" in order to resolve the pain in their lives. Instead, they need consistent, long-term support where their voices are not only heard, but empowered.

I have to admit that my own biases limited our growth as individuals and as a community because I did not realize that I was operating with a "white suburban evangelical Christian" checklist that defined who was qualified or good enough to work with our youth. I learned quickly that I had no business "speaking truth" into anyone else's life; in fact listening and learning were all I really had any business doing. Sadly, it took me a really long time to learn this lesson.

PATH TO RECIPROCITY

While this notion was important for me to grasp, I still didn't know how hard it would be to put it into action, specifically as it related to letting go of my need to voice my opinions. There remained an energy in me that always had an idea or a prescription for someone else's situation, and the youth I worked with in my early years tolerated way too much of my unsolicited advice. While I loved and supported them, I did not always truly listen, nor had I fully examined my identities and the worldview and privilege that they come with to make sure that the advice I gave was well-informed or even needed.

I did not understand how much I did not see or understand. Now, when I watch other white people interact with people outside their race or background, I recognize the same kind of well-intentioned, uninformed, and unsolicited sharing and advising when it happens. As white people, we tend to take up a lot of space in conversations and in relationships because we want to make sure our ideas and feelings are known. Sometimes we do this to the point that there isn't space for the ideas and feelings of others. In doing so we colonize these spaces, coming in without invitation, bringing all our ideas and expertise, and not seeing how we are perpetuating racism and op pression. We are so ready to save someone or lend a hand that we do not simply listen and learn.

For years I held down a full-time job in social work while mentoring youth and those parallel experiences taught me a lot. For me, the longer I worked in traditional social work, the more I felt conflicted about the ways our systems negatively impact those they attempt to serve, often people of color. Because our systems are often dominated by people of privilege, those of us who lead unexamined lives cannot see the ways our visions and perspectives can be limited and we often do not see the ways these systems do more harm than good to our most vulnerable communities.

Instead of meeting the actual needs of the people our systems purported to serve, I often saw youth being revictimized by dysfunctional systems where funding sources (or lack thereof) defined everything from the type of services provided to the quality of those services. And while the youth and families being served were almost exclusively people of color, most of the staff and upper management at many nonprofit organizations were not. When you are not from or representative of the community being served it is easy, intentionally or not, to make decisions that do not respect the culture or values of the community. It is often challenging to see the true strengths of the individuals or the community because we are looking through such a narrow lens. It is all too easy to fall into the trap of wanting to "fix' the community or individuals by making them more like ones of our own culture of origin. Services that were meant to help or heal often created new trauma. It is important to respect any community that one is serving enough to listen with humility, curiosity, and a deep intention to be of service in ways that best meet the needs of those being served.

Further, because organizations in the social services sector often employ young adults with minimal experience working for low wages, employee turnover was almost always high. People do good work with our youth but often only for a short season because, for self-serving or self-care reasons, they feel like they can't stay. What's lost here is the reality of the long-term consequences we create when we ask people to trust us and then we leave. It is not uncommon for youth to push through trauma and trust issues in order to form relationships with counselors, only to have that counselor leave after a very short time, moving on to graduate school or other employment, thus creating even more pain for the youth we intended to serve.

On a systems level, power dynamics need to be dismantled. People need to be served by people who can truly understand their experience and their struggle. Decisions that disproportionately impact people of color should not predominantly be made by people of a white, privileged background. This is why it is important that we elect leaders who truly understand and represent the communities they impact. The decision makers in our programs, non profits, schools, and churches should reflect the communities they walk alongside.

On a personal level, I realized I was contributing to the problem by not seeing the amazing resources right in front of me. What our youth from Oakland needed were more people from their own community who reflected their background and experiences. Did that mean people outside their race or background couldn't support them? Not in the least; but it did mean that we had a responsibility to be aware of the unnecessary obstacles that local leaders of color often face. White people - especially those in leadership - must stop taking up so much space and, instead, make room for local leaders to have voice and power in their own communities. Reciprocal relationships create space for mutual transformation and support.

MOVING FORWARD

For 19 years I have lived, loved and done life in East Oakland and I have always lived alongside our youth and families in the communities where they live. After years of mentoring youth I received a grant to grow the work, allowing me to step away from my social work career so I could instead focus on grassroot efforts to build a positive mentoring community that would help empower youth and adults to work together to better each other's lives and the greater community.

Now I grapple with what it means to a Director of this mentoring program, the Urban Mentors Network, in a community to which I am not indigenous and a community that does not reflect my racial or cultural background. I continue to feel conflicted that Oakland and communities like it are better when home grown leaders hold decision-making positions, leading through both practice and position. I know I must use my privilege to connect others to resources and opportunities they might not normally have access to, just as it is important to redirect the focus away from myself and onto the true unsung heroes that have held up places like Oakland for decades. Our communities of color are not lacking in amazing leaders; the parents, grandparents, alumni mentors, and others who come from this community have defined what our program has become. They should also be defining where the program should be going in the future.

Our society often celebrates the stories of people coming into a community that is not theirs to adopt children, teach inner city students, or fight for the lives of young gang members. We don't make movies about the mother in the neighborhood who takes care of her own children and others from the neighborhood as well. We don't make movies about how the community finds a way to collectively care of its own when outsiders leave or when funds get cut. All of us (Hollywood included) must change the narrative and shift the spotlights to the strong, beautiful and courageous souls who hold down these communities without outside gratitude or celebration. From here forward, that is my intention.

Oakland is a complicated, beautiful place filled with complicated, beautiful people and, as such, the obstacles people face here are not simple problems with simple solutions. Generational poverty, systemic racism, and inadequate resources are just a few layers of the complication. I am not the answer, nor am I a solution. At times I am even part of the problem.

I do need to do my part, as we all do, to open access to resources people should already have if we weren't operating in a country with oppression and racism at its core. In this time of rapid gentrification I am even more driven to empower the voices and visions of our youth and families to define our program. For me, this means listening to a diverse range of voices and opinions and making sure I don't allow my own cultural background or perspective to be what dominates the work we do. For someone else, it might start with taking an inventory of your social circle, your network, the books you read or the netflix you binge watch. It is so important that we take stock of what influences us and our viewpoints, and even more so, what limits our viewpoints. Maybe this month one starts with self-examination and choosing to step outside the normal comfort zone to read books or watch a documentary that addresses these hard issues or shares someone else's journey. Start watching, reading, and listening differently. LISTEN more and talk less. One of the things I also do is remind myself "I didn't choose institutional racism or the racism that is in me, but I must humbly work through it."

Those of us who come from privilege, especially from white privilege, need to stay grounded and humble. Addressing the racism within or around us improves our ability to make real change. We can make a difference, and no one needs our saving. What we need are open, honest, and reciprocal relationships. I call on all of us to create real space in our lives for folks who aren't like us and pay attention to the ways our perspectives are limited. We must realize that no matter how many relationships we have outside our race or how much anti-racism work we do, we are never done. Instead of claiming wokeness, we must wake up anew every day, seeking to grow, learn, and listen.

VI: LIVING INTO THE WORK

by Myisha T

T his is my story. I am not speaking for the collective divine feminine of black, brown or indigenous womxn, only for myself. The words may resonate or sound similar to what you or your friends' experiences may have been, but it is simply and profoundly my journey all its own. It is not to be dismissed or interpreted as speaking for others; instead, it is the offering of my lived experience guiding, living, and breathing the work.

I understand and recognize that it's hard for white women to dig into those dark spaces and actually see how subconscious and unconscious truths allow their actions to cause harm to Black and Indigenous People of Color. The difficulty calls all of us to go beyond the surface in order to dig deep into what I call Living into the Work. Living into stepping back. Living into owning your mistakes. Living into dismantling white supremacy in order to dismantle the systems that set BIPOC up to fail while simultaneously building a system and a world that allows us to succeed.

We have been socialized to believe that race experts are those with an extended post-secondary education. I realized for myself that I could no longer buy into that myth and the more the mindset of "I can't until I achieve ____" dissipated, the more I could live into the work. It's also given me the courage to stop coddling white women and, instead, support the recognition of our collective common humanity. I will no longer shy away from holding white women accountable for the way they show up in a relationship with BIPOC. I will also no longer shy away from the fact I am an expert in what it takes to do so.

It should come as no surprise that my experience as a woman of color in America is like the experience of other women of color who are minimized, shamed, and/or degraded for speaking their truths. Despite the risks, I will continue living this work in service to my children and their children. And I will not allow anyone who is willing to go on this journey with me, black or white, to be canceled for making mistakes.

I welcome anyone who cares to co-conspire with me against what bell hooks calls, "the white supremacist capitalist patriarchy." This is my story. And this is how Check Your Privilege was born.

ASSIMILATING NO MORE

We sat in a circle, deeply engaged in the work of my second Check Your Privilege workshop. Each woman was sharing how they understood their relationship with privilege and power, and what they could do about it. Then the question came up.

"How can I do this work as an educator? What can I do?" Jessica* asked.

Another woman, Karen*, stated, "Have you heard of Tim Wise? He works with educators and he is probably more palatable for you."

I felt the blood inside my body grow warm and my skin chill. This was not the first time a white woman had named an anti-racism professional from dominant culture as the "expert" on all things race. When this happened in previous workshops or calls with colleagues I silenced myself from saying anything; the "expert," the one who had written the book or had the degree, got my deference and those with whom I was working got my silence.

Since I had been working with my executive coach on power dynamics with white women and men, however, I knew deference and silence were no longer things I was willing to offer. That day would be the day I'd stand in my authority as an expert on this topic

"What makes you think it's acceptable to reference someone from the dominant culture outside this circle of work?" I asked. "I am a woman of color leading this session and in doing that you are denying my purpose in being here."

A palpable silence came over the circle of women. I could feel their fear, as if they assumed I was becoming the stereotypical angry black woman about to "go off."

But I didn't go off. And the group didn't retreat. Instead, within moments, Karen said, "You're right. I didn't think about it or about how it would make you feel. I apologize." This apology was one I'd wanted from white women for years. The white women who claimed, "I'm not racist," the ones who denied my experience, the Sunday school teacher who taught me to believe that Jesus didn't see color and therefore I shouldn't either.

After the workshop, I shared the implications of my decision to speak up with those closest to me and, together, we realized that I had claimed my power and legitimacy that day. I did not defer; I did not assimilate. I stood in my truth as a black woman, owning my words with love and standing in my knowledge with authority, something I had never been able to do before.

In anthropology and sociology circles, assimilation is "the process whereby individuals or groups of differing ethnic heritage are absorbed into the dominant culture of a society." Additionally, "the process of assimilating involves taking on the traits of the dominant culture to such a degree that the assimilating group becomes socially indistinguishable from other members of the society."

For me this means I am asked to put on a mask in order to survive dominant culture standards, taking on "a new persona" as Jung would say. As someone who appreciates being myself, it is hard for me to show up and perform for the sake of my livelihood but, because of the way I grew up, I became quite adept at it. This ability is both a gift and a curse: the gift of having a seat at the master's table and the curse of losing myself in the process. I've reached all the glass ceilings of perceived acceptance and success because I've shown myself as "non-threatening," participating quietly in white supremist culture, working twice as hard to get half as much.

I have been shamed for my teaching because of the perception that my style is not "good enough" for dominant culture standards. While I previously deferred to those standards--assimilation, credentials, and research--I now back up my work with something more powerful than all of those things: my lived experience with oppression and my experience with living into the work dismantling the systems that created it.

If I am to continue to live the work, and I am, I refuse to assimilate for the comfort of others any more.

REJECTING CANCEL CULTURE AND ITS ROOTS OF WHITE SUPREMACY

When it comes to Anti-Racism work I've seen people consistently choose to cancel each other versus looking to reconcile their differences. The role social media sometimes takes in activism is a perfect example of how this toxicity can perpetuate a patriarchal censoring of others, shutting down potentially well meaning co-conspirators before they even get started. We throw each other away rather than recognize our common humanity and the work it will take to collectively build an anti-racist society. Cancel culture is a symptom of a larger society built on white supremacy. White supremacy doesn't promote repair; instead it values separation, segregation and individualism.

In the spaces of activism, work, and anywhere the dominant culture reigns, women of color are told to sever their relationships with white women who cause harm. Although I understand it, this notion is out of alignment with the work I aim to do in the world. I brought the question to my executive coach, Valerie, to help me think about ways to (re)claim my power without throwing white women away. In previous coaching sessions Valerie had been able to name that I was looking for ways to share my lived harm from white women with white women. Knowing that many white women have come into my life and seen me as nothing more than their special project, I remember wondering how I could show up without shaming and victimizing other women.

My goal was two fold: one, to show that, even when white women make mistakes, behavior change is possible if they are given a chance; two, to empower women of color to be centered as the experts on conversations of race, power, and oppression instead of they typical "white allies" who almost always center whiteness.

"How can you take back your power?" Valerie asked.

"I've done lots of reading and work in therapy, and have realized that I don't want to throw white women away," I said.

"So, what do you want to do?" she asked.

"I want to interview white women and see how they're keeping their privilege in check so it doesn't impact the mental health of Black and Indigenous Women of Color."

"Okay, how will you do that?" Valerie asked.

"Mmm, I don't know, maybe interviews during minority Mental Health Awareness month? Who knows. I just know I'm doing something," I said.

Since I knew that my mental health had been impacted by unconscious bias and privilege, I decided to begin an interview series during minority Mental Health Awareness month called "Check Your Privilege." The idea was to interview white women in order to collectively inquire into what they were doing to keep their privilege in check in their relationships with Black and Indigenous Women of Color. I interviewed six white women and one Asian man, each ending the interview by asking me what they could do in order to continue to show up as better co-conspirators for People of Color.

Might this desire to take their engagement next-level be because I was clear that my intention was not to cancel them if they said something problematic, but to listen, inviting them into the space of co-conspiring together in service to what could be both for us as individuals and for our larger society?

In order to do this work I can't perpetuate the shame and blame narrative encouraged by cancel culture. If transformation is our goal, when "Annie," our hypothetical white woman, causes conscious/unconscious harm, we can't just cancel her; instead we have to shift the narrative from "Throw Annie Away," to "Let's be a guide for Annie on how to take personal responsibility for her behavior."

In a society based in the rugged individualism of patriarchy, it is easy for us to be unconscious participants in cancel culture. We see under-performing employees being thrown out of positions they could otherwise grow into, women getting fired for not giving "personal favors" to their male counterparts, and white women ending relationships with Women of Color who are no longer willing to serve them. In accepting any of these things, we are complicit in white supremacy. After those six interviews I knew I was no longer willing to comply.

Valerie and I started doing some real thinking about how I could use the Check Your Privilege brand to deepen the work through relationship and accountability. I had come to learn that everyone deserves a chance to change and, if I could walk alongside someone as a guide during their process, that collective healing would be possible. With my idea of using Check Your Privilege as a bridge to heal the divisiveness in the current anti-racist community, Valerie and I brainstormed coaching programs, community groups, book ideas, and workshops as ways to continue the work.

One year later, the Check Your Privilege brand grew to include an online membership space, a range of community workshops, and a collaborative book project. My intention was and continues to be transforming systemic white supremacy into power, purpose and the desire to live out of compassion and radical action.

CHOOSING CONSCIOUS RELATIONSHIPS

White supremacy teaches us that the thoughts, beliefs, and actions of the dominant culture are superior to those of people of color, but white people are not the only ones complicit in the adaptation of white supremacy. People of Color, who have asimilated in the patriarchal systems of oppression, also perform in a way that perpetuate the white supremacist narrative.

In 2001, Tema Okun and Kenneth Jones notated 15 characteristics of white supremacy in the Dismantling Racism Workbook. Those characteristics include but are not limited to "perfectionism, worship of written word, defensiveness, quality over quantity, paternalism, only one right way, right to comfort, power hoarding either or thinking, fear of open conflict, individualism, objectivity, progress is bigger, and I'm the only one." This list identifies how easy it is to adapt to dominant culture standards, which also translates into how easy it is to fall for it being the "best" way or the "only" way, but it is up to us to see how these standards impact the way we show up in relationship with one another.

We cause one another harm when we are unconscious, whether that be unconsciously holding each other to the standards of dominant culture or unconsciously playing out our intergenerational trauma onto one another. For example when a white male supervisor treats a female employee poorly, she will transfer residual trauma to other women, silencing them, perhaps, for speaking their truths. A white woman who was silenced will, in turn, silence a woman of color, who will, in turn, go on to pass her residual pain on to another who comes after her. This cycle can be seen time and time again, across time and space and generations, playing out in our workplaces and our schools and our lives, perpetuating both historical and modern-day harm and disdain.

Being silenced for speaking my truth to white women is what empowered Check Your Privilege in the first place, because the moment I try to state a boundary in a relationship I am often called out, shamed into silence, or for lack of better words, put "out into my place." The idea that I, as a Woman of Color, could not have boundaries, led me to believe that, without boundaries, especially in intercultural relationships, the roots of white supremacy will continue to perpetuate an endless cycle of harm. I refuse to be a part of that problem anymore

The call to live into the work is a call into conscious relationships. In a world filled with spiritual bypassing and toxic positivity, we have learned it's easier to throw relationships away rather than working towards repair and reconciliation. As someone who believes in restorative repair in relationships, I'm not interested in throwing any woman away, and I do have to remember my boundaries because many white women, if they feel forced to choose, will choose race over gender every time.

I understand and recognize that it's hard for white women to dig into the dark spaces and actually see how subconscious and unconscious truths allow their actions to cause harm to Black, Brown and Indigenous People of Color. I also realize it's not just doing the work that's important, rather it's about Living into the Work. Living into stepping back. Living into owning your mistakes. Living into dismantling white supremacist capitalist patriarchy in order to demolish the systems that set BIPOC up to fail, while rebuilding a system that allows us to succeed. What I know for sure is that I am an expert in this work because I am shaped by my life experience every day and, instead of throwing people away, I choose to live into the work.

I welcome anyone who cares to co-conspire with me.

ABOUT THE
Contributors

Heather Anderson

HEATHER ANDERSON

is the Founder of "The Mama-hood," the largest and most diverse support group for mothers in the San Francis-co Bay Area, as well as "The Club," a community for womxn entrepreneurs. With an intention to moderate her online forums through a lens of social justice, she leans heavily into the work of checking her own white privilege while guiding her members on the same journey. Her talk, "Social Justice Within Online Communities: How to Moderate for Diversity and Inclusion" was featured at Facebook's Community Summit 2019 to community leaders from around the world. In addition to being a serial entrepreneur, Heather is a speaker, songwriter, bandleader, partner, and mother of five with a love for graphic novels and a penchant for reading cookbooks without actually doing the cooking.

Learn more about Heather
at <u>heatherlynnanderson.com</u> and <u>themamahood.com</u>

JAIME BLANCO

Jaime Blanco

Born in Ann Arbor, Michigan, Jaime Blanco has lived in Oakland, California for the past 19 years and is the founder and director of Urban Mentors Network, an East Oakland based mentoring program focused on building a safe empowering community where youth and adults form reciprocal relationships, always learning from one another. Jaime is recently married, the proud mama of her two beautiful pit bulls, Nina & Layla, and is extremely grateful to have a diverse circle of friends and family who keep her honest and help balance her perspectives.

Learn more about Jaime and the Urban Mentors Network at urbanmentors.org

Jennifer Kinney

JENNIFER KINNEY

is a writer, podcaster, mother, wife, and activist. She loves to travel the world and learn about different cultures, particularly through their food. She is an avid reader, though her pile of unread books would indicate she is more of a collector at this point. She spent 15 years educating people about the realities of human trafficking and worked in communications for a non-profit anti-trafficking organization in Asia. Jen believes in the power and importance of human connection and created Food For Thought Dinner Parties, where she gathers people for good food and difficult conversations. In 2012, after the killing of Trayvon Martin, she began digging deeper into the topic of race in the US and started her journey into anti-racism. She discovered her love for podcasting in 2018 and is the host of Speaking of Racism Podcast.

Learn more about Jen and her podcast
at <u>jenkinney.com</u> and <u>speakingofracism.com</u>

BRITNEY STAFFORD

is a music lover of many genres, writes as an emotional outlet, and loves painting with her son. She is happily married and she and her husband are the obnoxiously proud parents of a funny, energetic, and caring six year-old. Originally from Wisconsin, she now lives with her family in Georgia. She is a huge animal lover with nine (yes, nine!) cats and one dog. Britney is a homeschool mom and social media marketer who also enjoys volunteering in her community. She is a proponent of human connection and mental health. She says that her core beliefs, the experiences of friends and strangers, and the undeniable truths about racism and white supremacy, along with the support and guidance of others have led her on a journey towards anti-racism.

Learn more about Britney at <u>britneystafford.com</u>

MYISHA T

Founder of the Check Your Privilege movement and contributor and Editor of the Check Your Privilege anthology, Myisha T. Hill is a human-design generator and MBTi ENFJ with action-oriented justice in her blood. A single mom of 3 differently abled children, Myisha is also a mental health advocate, and social entrepreneur. An advocate for healing and social transformation, Myisha continues to center the work of Check Your Privilege from a mental health perspective, using self-compassion practices and reflection to help white folx step back, reflect, and compassionately dismantle their relationship with power, privilege, and oppression. When she's not guiding the practice of those engaged with Check Your Privilege, Myisha lives her role as a mental health advocate to facilitate wellness workshops and peer support groups with black, brown and indgenious womxn through a restorative justice project she founded and sponsors called, Brown Sisters Speak.

Learn more about Myisha at <u>myishat.com</u>
@iammyishat & @ckyourprivilege on Instagram

BRANDY VARNADO

Brandy Varnado

is a mother, educator and entrepreneur living in the Bay Area. She began a career in education over 13 years ago in an effort to give back to her community and is most passionate about equipping individuals with the tools and skills necessary to create economic opportunities for themselves through education and developing an entrepreneurial mindset. A serial entrepreneur herself, she is the creator of The Black Market Group, a natural boutique skincare brand, as well as a portrait photographer. Throughout her career she has sought to engage in conversations at the intersection of race and opportunity, pushing for practices that are deeply rooted in equity.

Learn more about Brandy on Instagram @brandywashere, LinkedIn @brandyvarnado, and her website, brandywashere.com

To learn more about

CHECK YOUR PRIVILEGE

visit

CHECKYOURPRIVILEGE.CO

CPSIA information can be obtained
at www.ICGtesting.com
Printed in the USA
LVHW031201020620
657221LV00022B/1486